Master JavaScript in 30 Days

Rebecca Cox

Published by Rebecca Cox, 2023.

MASTER JAVASCRIPT IN 30 DAYS

First edition. July 2, 2023.

Copyright © 2023 Rebecca Cox.

ISBN: 979-8223763130

Written by Rebecca Cox.

Table of Contents

Introduction

Welcome to "Master JavaScript in 30 Days," a comprehensive guide designed to help you gain a deep understanding of JavaScript within a month.

Whether you're a beginner or an experienced developer looking to enhance your skills, this book will provide you with the knowledge and hands-on practice necessary to become a JavaScript master.

By dedicating time each day to studying and practicing JavaScript, you'll unlock the full potential of this powerful programming language and become proficient in creating dynamic and interactive web applications.

So, let's embark on this exciting journey together!

Day 1: Getting Started with JavaScript

Welcome to Day 1 of "Master JavaScript in 30 Days".

Today, we'll begin our journey by getting acquainted with JavaScript and setting up our development environment.

Let's get to it!

Topics Covered:

1. Introduction to JavaScript

2. Setting up the Development Environment

3. Writing Your First JavaScript Code

4. Understanding Variables and Data Types

Introduction to JavaScript:

JavaScript is a high-level, interpreted programming language primarily used for adding interactivity and dynamic behavior to web pages. It enables developers to create engaging user interfaces, perform calculations, manipulate data, and interact with web APIs. JavaScript is supported by all major web browsers, making it a fundamental language for web development.

Setting up the Development Environment:

To get started with JavaScript development, you need a text editor and a web browser. Popular text editors include Visual Studio Code, Sublime Text, and Atom. Choose the one you're comfortable with, and make sure it has JavaScript syntax highlighting and other useful extensions.

For running and testing JavaScript code, any modern web browser will do. Chrome, Firefox, or Safari are recommended choices. They come with powerful developer tools that aid in debugging and inspecting web applications.

Writing Your First JavaScript Code:

Let's write our first JavaScript code! Create a new file with a ".js" extension, such as "hello.js." Open the file in your text editor and add the following code:

```
console.log("Hello, JavaScript!");
```

Save the file and open it in your web browser. Open the browser's developer console by right-clicking on the page, selecting "Inspect" or "Inspect Element," and navigating to the "Console" tab. You should see the message "Hello, JavaScript!" printed in the console.

Congratulations! You've successfully executed your first JavaScript code. The `console.log()` function is used to display messages or data in the browser's console.

Understanding Variables and Data Types:

Variables are containers used to store data values in JavaScript. They provide a way to refer to these values and manipulate them throughout your code. JavaScript has several built-in data types, including:

1. Numbers: Used for numeric values, such as 5, 3.14, or -10.

2. Strings: Represented by text enclosed in single or double quotes, such as "Hello" or 'JavaScript'.

3. Booleans: Represent either `true` or `false` and are used in logical operations.

To declare a variable, use the `var`, `let`, or `const` keyword, followed by the variable name. For example:

```
var age = 25;
```

```
let name = "John";
```

```
const PI = 3.14159;
```

The `var` keyword is used to declare variables with function scope, while `let` and `const` are used for block scope. `const` creates a constant variable whose value cannot be changed once assigned.

Now it's your turn to practice!

Declare a variable called `message` and assign it a string value of your choice. Print the value of `message` to the console using `console.log()`.

```
let message = "Welcome to JavaScript!";
```

```
console.log(message);
```

Save the file, refresh the web page, and check the console to see your message displayed.

That wraps up Day 1!

Today, you learned about JavaScript, set up your development environment, wrote your first JavaScript code, and explored variables and data types. Tomorrow, we'll dive deeper into operators and expressions. Keep up the great work, and see you in Day 2.

Day 2: Working with Operators and Expressions

Welcome to Day 2 of "Master JavaScript in 30 Days".

Today, we'll explore the world of operators and expressions in JavaScript. These fundamental building blocks allow us to perform calculations, manipulate data, and make decisions in our code.

Topics Covered:

1. Arithmetic Operators

2. Assignment Operators

3. Comparison Operators

4. Logical Operators

Arithmetic Operators:

Arithmetic operators are used to perform mathematical calculations in JavaScript. Here are the commonly used arithmetic operators:

1. Addition (+): Adds two values together.

2. Subtraction (-): Subtracts one value from another.

3. Multiplication (*): Multiplies two values.

4. Division (/): Divides one value by another.

5. Modulo (%): Returns the remainder of a division operation.

6. Increment (++) and Decrement (—): Increases or decreases a value by 1.

Let's explore these operators with some examples:

let a = 10;

let b = 5;

let sum = a + b;

```javascript
console.log("Sum:", sum);

let difference = a - b;

console.log("Difference:", difference);

let product = a * b;

console.log("Product:", product);

let quotient = a / b;

console.log("Quotient:", quotient);

let remainder = a % b;

console.log("Remainder:", remainder);

a++; // Increment a by 1

console.log("Incremented a:", a);

b—; // Decrement b by 1

console.log("Decremented b:", b);
```

Assignment Operators:

Assignment operators are used to assign values to variables. They combine the assignment (=) operator with other arithmetic operators. Here are some examples:

```javascript
let x = 10;

x += 5; // Equivalent to: x = x + 5

console.log("Updated x:", x);

x -= 3; // Equivalent to: x = x - 3

console.log("Updated x:", x);

x *= 2; // Equivalent to: x = x * 2

console.log("Updated x:", x);
```

```
x /= 4; // Equivalent to: x = x / 4
```

```
console.log("Updated x:", x);
```

```
x %= 2; // Equivalent to: x = x % 2
```

```
console.log("Updated x:", x);
```

Comparison Operators:

Comparison operators are used to compare values and return a Boolean (true or false) result. They are often used in conditional statements and loops. Here are the commonly used comparison operators:

1. Equal to (==): Checks if two values are equal.

2. Not equal to (!=): Checks if two values are not equal.

3. Greater than (>): Checks if the left value is greater than the right value.

4. Less than (<): Checks if the left value is less than the right value.

5. Greater than or equal to (>=): Checks if the left value is greater than or equal to the right value.

6. Less than or equal to (<=): Checks if the left value is less than or equal to the right value.

Let's see some examples:

```
let num1 = 10;
```

```
let num2 = 5;
```

```
console.log(num1 == num2); // false
```

```
console.log(num1 != num2); // true
```

```
console.log(num1 > num2); // true
```

```
console.log(num1 < num2); // false
```

```
console.log(num1 >= num2); // true
```

```
console.log(num1 <= num2); // false
```

Logical Operators:

Logical operators are used to combine or modify logical conditions. They return a Boolean value based on the truth or falsity of the operands. Here are

the logical operators in JavaScript:

1. Logical AND (&&): Returns true if both operands are true.

2. Logical OR (||): Returns true if either operand is true.

3. Logical NOT (!): Reverses the logical state of an operand.

Let's see how they work:

let x = 5;

let y = 10;

let z = 15;

console.log(x < y && y < z); // true

console.log(x > y || y < z); // true

console.log(!(x > y)); // true

That wraps up Day 2!

Today, we explored arithmetic operators, assignment operators, comparison operators, and logical operators. These powerful tools allow us to perform calculations and make decisions in our JavaScript code. Tomorrow, we'll dive into control flow and decision making with conditional statements. Keep up the great work, and see you in Day 3.

Day 3: Control Flow and Decision Making

Welcome to Day 3 of "Master JavaScript in 30 Days".

Today, we'll delve into control flow and decision making in JavaScript. These concepts allow us to execute different blocks of code based on certain conditions. Let's explore conditional statements and loops!

Topics Covered:

1. Conditional Statements: if, else if, else

2. Switch Statements

3. Loops: for, while, do-while

4. Break and Continue Statements

Conditional Statements: if, else if, else

Conditional statements allow us to execute different blocks of code based on specified conditions. The most commonly used conditional statement is the `if` statement. It evaluates a condition, and if the condition is true, the associated block of code is executed. If the condition is false, the code block is skipped.

Here's an example:

let num = 10;

if (num > 0) {

console.log("The number is positive.");

}

In this example, if the value of `num` is greater than 0, the message "The number is positive" will be printed to the console.

We can also include an `else` statement to specify a block of code to be executed if the condition is false:

```
let num = -5;

if (num > 0) {

console.log("The number is positive.");

} else {

console.log("The number is not positive.");

}
```

In this case, if the value of `num` is not greater than 0, the message "The number is not positive" will be printed.

Additionally, we can use the `else if` statement to evaluate multiple conditions:

```
let num = 0;

if (num > 0) {

console.log("The number is positive.");

} else if (num < 0) {

console.log("The number is negative.");

} else {

console.log("The number is zero.");

}
```

In this example, if the value of `num` is greater than 0, "The number is positive" is printed. If `num` is less than 0, "The number is negative" is printed. Otherwise, if `num` is neither greater nor less than 0, "The number is zero" is printed.

Switch Statements:

Switch statements provide an alternative way to handle multiple conditions. They evaluate an expression and execute the code block that corresponds to a specific case.

Here's an example:

```javascript
let day = "Monday";

switch (day) {

case "Monday":

console.log("It's the beginning of the week.");

break;

case "Friday":

console.log("It's the end of the week.");

break;

default:

console.log("It's another day.");

break;

}
```

In this example, the code block associated with the matching case will be executed. If `day` is "Monday," the message "It's the beginning of the week" will be printed. If `day` is "Friday," the message "It's the end of the week" will be printed. If neither condition is met, the `default` block will be executed.

Loops: for, while, do-while

Loops allow us to execute a block of code repeatedly. JavaScript provides several loop structures, including `for`, `while`, and `do-while`.

The `for` loop is commonly used when the number of iterations is known:

```javascript
for (let i = 0; i < 5; i++) {

console.log("Iteration", i);

}
```

In this example, the loop will iterate five times, and the message "Iteration" followed by the current value of `i` will be printed to the console.

The `while` loop is used when the number of iterations is not known in advance:

```
let i = 0;

while (i < 5) {

console.log("Iteration", i);

i++;

}
```

This loop will continue to execute as long as the condition `i < 5` is true. Once `i` becomes 5 or greater, the loop will terminate.

The `do-while` loop is similar to the `while` loop but guarantees that the code block is executed at least once before the condition is checked:

```
let i = 0;

do {

console.log("Iteration", i);

i++;

} while (i < 5);
```

In this example, the code block is executed first, and then the condition `i < 5` is evaluated. If the condition is true, the loop will continue. Otherwise, it will terminate.

Break and Continue Statements:

The `break` statement is used to exit a loop prematurely:

```
for (let i = 0; i < 10; i++) {

if (i === 5) {

break;

}
```

```
console.log("Iteration", i);

}
```

In this example, when `i` becomes 5, the loop will be terminated, and the code execution will move to the next statement outside the loop.

The `continue` statement is used to skip the current iteration and move to the next iteration:

```
for (let i = 0; i < 10; i++) {

if (i % 2 === 0) {

continue;

}

console.log("Odd number:", i);

}
```

In this example, when `i` is an even number, the `continue` statement is encountered, and the loop skips to the next iteration without executing the remaining code block.

That wraps up Day 3!

Today, we explored conditional statements (if, else if, else), switch statements, loops (for, while, do-while), and break and continue statements. These control flow structures empower us to make decisions and execute code repeatedly in JavaScript. Tomorrow, we'll dive into arrays and their manipulation. Keep up the great work, and see you in Day 4.

Day 4: Arrays and Array Manipulation

Welcome to Day 4 of "Master JavaScript in 30 Days"! Today, we'll dive into arrays, one of the most fundamental data structures in JavaScript. Arrays allow us to store and manipulate collections of data. Let's explore arrays and learn how to work with them effectively.

Topics Covered:

1. Introduction to Arrays

2. Creating and Accessing Arrays

3. Modifying Arrays

4. Array Methods

Introduction to Arrays:

An array is a data structure that allows us to store multiple values in a single variable. Arrays can hold elements of any data type, such as numbers, strings, objects, or even other arrays. They provide us with a convenient way to organize and manipulate related data.

Creating and Accessing Arrays:

To create an array, we use square brackets [] and separate the elements with commas. Here's an example:

let fruits = ["apple", "banana", "orange", "mango"];

In this example, we've created an array called `fruits` that contains four elements: "apple", "banana", "orange", and "mango".

We can access individual elements in an array using their index. The index starts from 0 for the first element, 1 for the second element, and so on. For example:

console.log(fruits[0]); // "apple"

console.log(fruits[2]); // "orange"

In this case, `fruits[0]` retrieves the first element ("apple"), and `fruits[2]` retrieves the third element ("orange").

Modifying Arrays:

Arrays are mutable, meaning we can change their elements after they're created. We can modify elements by assigning new values to specific indices. Here's an example:

let numbers = [1, 2, 3, 4, 5];

numbers[2] = 10;

console.log(numbers); // [1, 2, 10, 4, 5]

In this example, `numbers[2]` is assigned the new value of 10, modifying the original array.

Array Methods:

JavaScript provides a variety of built-in methods that make working with arrays more convenient. Let's explore some commonly used array methods:

1. `push()`: Adds one or more elements to the end of an array.

let fruits = ["apple", "banana"];

fruits.push("orange", "mango");

console.log(fruits); // ["apple", "banana", "orange", "mango"]

2. `pop()`: Removes the last element from an array and returns it.

let fruits = ["apple", "banana", "orange", "mango"];

let removedFruit = fruits.pop();

console.log(fruits); // ["apple", "banana", "orange"]

console.log(removedFruit); // "mango"

3. `shift()`: Removes the first element from an array and returns it.

let fruits = ["apple", "banana", "orange"];

let removedFruit = fruits.shift();

console.log(fruits); // ["banana", "orange"]

```
console.log(removedFruit); // "apple"
```

4. `unshift()`: Adds one or more elements to the beginning of an array.

```
let fruits = ["banana", "orange"];
```

```
fruits.unshift("apple", "mango");
```

```
console.log(fruits); // ["apple", "mango", "banana", "orange"]
```

5. `slice()`: Returns a new array containing a portion of the original array.

```
let numbers = [1, 2, 3, 4
```

```
, 5];
```

```
let slicedNumbers = numbers.slice(1, 4);
```

```
console.log(slicedNumbers); // [2, 3, 4]
```

These are just a few examples of the many array methods available in JavaScript. They provide powerful ways to manipulate and transform arrays.

That wraps up Day 4!

Today, we explored arrays, including creating and accessing them, modifying their elements, and using array methods for manipulation. Arrays are essential in JavaScript, and understanding how to work with them effectively is crucial. Tomorrow, we'll dive into functions, one of the most important concepts in JavaScript. Keep up the great work, and see you in Day 5.

Day 5: Functions and Function Declarations

Welcome to Day 5 of "Master JavaScript in 30 Days"!

Today, we'll explore functions, one of the most crucial concepts in JavaScript. Functions allow us to encapsulate reusable blocks of code and execute them whenever needed. Let's dive into functions and learn how to declare and use them effectively.

Topics Covered:

1. Introduction to Functions

2. Function Declarations

3. Function Parameters and Arguments

4. Returning Values from Functions

Introduction to Functions:

In JavaScript, a function is a block of code that performs a specific task or calculates a value. Functions provide modularity and reusability in our code by encapsulating a set of instructions that can be invoked multiple times. They allow us to organize and structure our code logically.

Function Declarations:

A function declaration is the most common way to define a function in JavaScript. It consists of the `function` keyword followed by the function name, a set of parentheses for optional parameters, and a code block enclosed in curly braces. Here's an example:

```
function greet() {

console.log("Hello, welcome to Day 5 of JavaScript!");

}
```

In this example, we've defined a function called `greet` that logs a greeting message to the console.

To execute a function and run the code inside it, we use the function name followed by parentheses. Here's how we invoke the `greet` function:

```
greet();
```

When we invoke the function using `greet()`, the code inside the function block is executed, and the greeting message is printed to the console.

Function Parameters and Arguments:

Functions can accept inputs called parameters. Parameters act as placeholders for values that we can pass to the function when invoking it. Here's an example:

```
function greet(name) {

console.log("Hello, " + name + "! Welcome to Day 5 of JavaScript!");

}
```

In this modified `greet` function, we've added a parameter called `name`. The function will use this parameter to personalize the greeting message.

When invoking a function with parameters, we pass specific values called arguments. Here's how we pass an argument to the `greet` function:

```
greet("John");
```

In this example, we're passing the string `"John"` as an argument to the `greet` function. The function will use this value to customize the greeting message.

Returning Values from Functions:

Functions can also return values using the `return` statement. The returned value can be assigned to a variable or used directly in other parts of the code. Here's an example:

```
function add(a, b) {

return a + b;

}
```

In this example, the `add` function takes two parameters `a` and `b` and returns their sum.

We can capture the returned value by assigning it to a variable:

```
let result = add(5, 3);
```

```
console.log(result); // 8
```

In this case, the `add` function is invoked with arguments 5 and 3, and the returned value of 8 is stored in the `result` variable.

That wraps up Day 5!

Today, we explored functions and function declarations in JavaScript. Functions provide a way to encapsulate reusable code blocks and execute them when needed. We learned how to define functions, use parameters and arguments, and return values from functions. Tomorrow, we'll dive into function expressions and explore more advanced concepts. Keep up the great work, and see you in Day 6.

Day 6: Function Expressions & Higher-Order Functions

Welcome to Day 6 of "Master JavaScript in 30 Days"!

Today, we'll continue our exploration of functions by diving into function expressions and higher-order functions. These concepts allow us to create more flexible and powerful functions in JavaScript.

Topics Covered:

1. Function Expressions

2. Anonymous Functions

3. Higher-Order Functions

4. Callback Functions

Function Expressions:

In addition to function declarations, JavaScript also allows us to define functions using function expressions. Function expressions involve assigning a function to a variable. Here's an example:

let greet = function() {

console.log("Hello, welcome to Day 6 of JavaScript!");

};

In this example, we've defined a function expression and assigned it to a variable called `greet`. The function doesn't have a name and is created as an anonymous function.

We can invoke the function expression using the variable name followed by parentheses, just like we do with function declarations:

greet();

Anonymous Functions:

Anonymous functions are function expressions without a specified name. They are commonly used in situations where we need to define a function on the fly or pass a function as an argument to another function. Here's an example:

```
let square = function(num) {

return num * num;

};

console.log(square(5)); // 25
```

In this example, we've defined an anonymous function expression called `square`. It takes a parameter `num` and returns the square of that number.

Higher-Order Functions:

A higher-order function is a function that operates on other functions. It can accept functions as arguments, return functions, or both. Higher-order functions provide a way to create more flexible and reusable code. Here's an example:

```
function greet(name) {

console.log("Hello, " + name + "!");

}

function higherOrderGreet(callback) {

let userName = "John";

callback(userName);

}

higherOrderGreet(greet); // Outputs: "Hello, John!"
```

In this example, we have a higher-order function called `higherOrderGreet` that accepts a callback function as an argument. Inside the `higherOrderGreet` function, we define a variable `userName` and pass it as an argument when invoking the callback function.

Callback Functions:

A callback function is a function passed as an argument to another function and is invoked inside that function. Callback functions allow us to execute specific code at a later time or in response to certain events. Here's an example:

```
function processArray(array, callback) {

for (let i = 0; i < array.length; i++) {

callback(array[i]);

}

}

function logElement(element) {

console.log(element);

}

let numbers = [1, 2, 3, 4, 5];

processArray(numbers, logElement); // Outputs: 1, 2, 3, 4, 5
```

In this example, we have a function `processArray` that accepts an array and a callback function as arguments. Inside the `processArray` function, we iterate over each element of the array and invoke the callback function for each element.

That wraps up Day 6!

Today, we explored function expressions, anonymous functions, higher-order functions, and callback functions. These concepts expand our capabilities in creating flexible and reusable code. Tomorrow, we'll dive into object-oriented programming in JavaScript. Keep up the great work, and see you in Day 7.

Day 7: Object-Oriented Programming in JavaScript

Welcome to Day 7 of "Master JavaScript in 30 Days"!

Today, we'll explore object-oriented programming (OOP) in JavaScript. OOP is a programming paradigm that allows us to model real-world entities as objects with properties and behaviors. JavaScript provides several features that enable us to implement OOP concepts effectively.

Topics Covered:

1. Objects in JavaScript

2. Creating Objects

3. Object Properties and Methods

4. Constructor Functions and the 'new' Keyword

Objects in JavaScript:

In JavaScript, objects are the core building blocks of OOP. An object is a collection of key-value pairs, where the keys are called properties and the values can be any data type or even other objects. Objects allow us to organize related data and behavior into a single entity.

Creating Objects:

There are multiple ways to create objects in JavaScript. One of the common approaches is using object literals, which involves defining objects directly with curly braces {}. Here's an example:

```
let person = {

name: "John",

age: 30,

greet: function() {

console.log("Hello, my name is " + this.name + "!");

}

};
```

In this example, we've created an object called `person` with properties like `name` and `age`. The `greet` property contains a function that logs a greeting message using the object's name property.

Object Properties and Methods:

Objects can have properties, which are variables that hold values, and methods, which are functions that perform actions or calculations. We can access object properties and invoke methods using dot notation or square brackets. Here are some examples:

console.log(person.name); // "John"

console.log(person.age); // 30

person.greet(); // Outputs: "Hello, my name is John!"

In these examples, we access the `name` and `age` properties using dot notation (`object.property`). We also invoke the `greet` method using dot notation (`object.method()`).

Constructor Functions and the 'new' Keyword:

Constructor functions are special functions in JavaScript that are used to create objects of a specific type or class. They are typically named with an initial uppercase letter to indicate their purpose. Constructor functions are used in combination with the `new` keyword to create new instances of objects. Here's an example:

function Person(name, age) {

this.name = name;

this.age = age;

this.greet = function() {

console.log("Hello, my name is " + this.name + "!");

};

}

let person1 = new Person("John", 30);

let person2 = new Person("Jane", 25);

person1.greet(); // Outputs: "Hello, my name is John!"

person2.greet(); // Outputs: "Hello, my name is Jane!"

In this example, we define a constructor function called `Person` with `name` and `age` parameters. Inside the constructor function, we use the `this` keyword to refer to the current object being created. We assign the passed arguments to object properties and define the `greet` method.

To create new instances of the `Person` object, we use the `new` keyword followed by the constructor function name and provide the necessary arguments.

That wraps up Day 7!

Today, we explored object-oriented programming in JavaScript, including creating objects, defining properties and methods, and using constructor functions. OOP is a powerful paradigm that allows us to structure our code in a more organized and reusable manner. Tomorrow, we'll delve into inheritance and prototypes. Keep up the great work, and see you in Day 8.

Day 8: Prototypes and Inheritance

Welcome to Day 8 of "Master JavaScript in 30 Days"!

Today, we'll continue our exploration of object-oriented programming in JavaScript by diving into prototypes and inheritance. These concepts allow us to create relationships between objects and share properties and methods.

Topics Covered:

1. Prototypes in JavaScript

2. The Prototype Chain

3. Inheritance using Prototypes

4. Creating Subclasses

Prototypes in JavaScript:

In JavaScript, every object has an internal link to another object called its prototype. The prototype is an object from which the current object inherits properties and methods. Prototypes allow us to create relationships and share behavior between objects efficiently.

The Prototype Chain:

JavaScript implements a prototype chain, which is a mechanism for searching properties and methods in an object's prototype and its prototype's prototype, and so on, until the property or method is found or until the end of the chain is reached.

To access the prototype of an object, we use the `Object.getPrototypeOf()` method or the `__proto__` property. Here's an example:

let person = {

name: "John",

age: 30,

};

```javascript
let prototype = Object.getPrototypeOf(person);

console.log(prototype); // Outputs: {}
```

In this example, we use `Object.getPrototypeOf()` to retrieve the prototype of the `person` object. Since we haven't explicitly set a prototype, it returns an empty object `{}`.

Inheritance using Prototypes:

Prototypes enable us to achieve inheritance in JavaScript. By assigning an object as the prototype of another object, we can inherit properties and methods from the prototype object. Here's an example:

```javascript
let personPrototype = {

greet: function() {

console.log("Hello, my name is " + this.name + "!");

}

};

let person = Object.create(personPrototype);

person.name = "John";

person.age = 30;

person.greet(); // Outputs: "Hello, my name is John!"
```

In this example, we define an object `personPrototype` that serves as the prototype for the `person` object. The `Object.create()` method is used to create a new object with the specified prototype. We then assign properties to the `person` object and invoke the `greet` method, which is inherited from the prototype.

Creating Subclasses:

In JavaScript, we can create subclasses, which are objects that inherit from a parent object or class. Subclasses can add or override properties and methods from their parent. Here's an example:

```javascript
function Employee(name, age, position) {

this.name = name;
```

```javascript
this.age = age;

this.position = position;

}

Employee.prototype.greet = function() {

console.log("Hello, my name is " + this.name + "!");

};

function Manager(name, age, position, department) {

Employee.call(this, name, age, position);

this.department = department;

}

Manager.prototype = Object.create(Employee.prototype);

Manager.prototype.constructor = Manager;

Manager.prototype.manage = function() {

console.log("I am managing the " + this.department + " department.");

};

let manager = new Manager("John", 35, "Manager", "Sales");

manager.greet(); // Outputs: "Hello, my name is John!"

manager.manage(); // Outputs: "I am managing the Sales department."
```

In this example, we have an `Employee` constructor function that sets the basic properties and defines the `greet` method. The `Manager` constructor function inherits from `Employee` using `Object.create()` and adds a new property `department` and the `manage` method.

We set the prototype of `Manager` to be an object that inherits from `Employee.prototype`. Additionally, we ensure that the `constructor` property of `Manager.prototype` is correctly set.

That wraps up Day 8!

Today, we explored prototypes and inheritance in JavaScript. Prototypes allow us to create relationships between objects and share properties and methods efficiently. We also learned how to create subclasses and extend the functionality of parent objects. Tomorrow, we'll dive into JavaScript modules and how to organize our code effectively. Keep up the great work, and see you in Day 9.

Day 9: JavaScript Modules

Welcome to Day 9 of "Master JavaScript in 30 Days"!

Today, we'll explore JavaScript modules, a powerful feature that allows us to organize our code into reusable and maintainable units. Modules enable us to encapsulate functionality, manage dependencies, and promote code modularity.

Topics Covered:

1. Introduction to JavaScript Modules

2. Exporting and Importing Modules

3. CommonJS Modules

4. ES Modules

Introduction to JavaScript Modules:

A module is a self-contained unit of code that encapsulates related functionality, such as variables, functions, classes, or objects. Modules allow us to break our code into smaller, reusable parts, making it easier to understand, maintain, and collaborate with others.

Exporting and Importing Modules:

In JavaScript, we can export and import modules to access their functionality in other parts of our code.

To export elements from a module, we use the `export` keyword. There are different ways to export elements, such as variables, functions, or classes. Here's an example:

```
// math.js

export const PI = 3.14159;

export function add(a, b) {

return a + b;

}

export class Circle {
```

```
constructor(radius) {

this.radius = radius;

}

calculateArea() {

return PI * this.radius * this.radius;

}

}
```

In this example, we export a constant `PI`, a function `add`, and a class `Circle` from the `math.js` module.

To import elements from a module, we use the `import` keyword. We can import specific elements or use the `*` symbol to import all exported elements. Here's an example:

```
// main.js

import { add, Circle } from './math.js';

console.log(add(2, 3)); // Outputs: 5

const circle = new Circle(5);

console.log(circle.calculateArea()); // Outputs: 78.53975
```

In this example, we import the `add` function and the `Circle` class from the `math.js` module using destructuring. We can then use these imported elements in our code.

CommonJS Modules:

CommonJS is a module system used in Node.js and other environments. CommonJS modules use the `require()` function to import modules and the `module.exports` or `exports` object to export functionality. Here's an example:

```
// math.js

const PI = 3.14159;
```

```javascript
function add(a, b) {
return a + b;
}
class Circle {
constructor(radius) {
this.radius = radius;
}
calculateArea() {
return PI * this.radius * this.radius;
}
}
module.exports = {
PI,
add,
Circle
};
```

In this example, we use `module.exports` to export the `PI`, `add`, and `Circle` elements from the `math.js` module.

To import these elements in another module, we use the `require()` function. Here's an example:

```javascript
// main.js
const { add, Circle } = require('./math.js');
console.log(add(2, 3)); // Outputs: 5
const circle = new Circle(5);
```

console.log(circle.calculateArea()); // Outputs: 78.53975

ES Modules:

ES Modules (ESM) are the standard module system in modern JavaScript. They use the `import` and `export` keywords to handle module imports and exports. ES modules are supported in modern browsers and can be used with tools like webpack or Babel to ensure compatibility. Here's an example:

```
// math.js

const

PI = 3.14159;

function add(a, b) {

return a + b;

}

export class Circle {

constructor(radius) {

this.radius = radius;

}

calculateArea() {

return PI * this.radius * this.radius;

}

}

export { PI, add };
```

In this example, we export the `PI`, `add`, and `Circle` elements using the `export` keyword.

To import these elements in another module, we use the `import` keyword. Here's an example:

```
// main.js
```

```
import { add, Circle } from './math.js';

console.log(add(2, 3)); // Outputs: 5

const circle = new Circle(5);

console.log(circle.calculateArea()); // Outputs: 78.53975
```

In this example, we import the `add` function and the `Circle` class from the `math.js` module using destructuring.

That wraps up Day 9!

Today, we explored JavaScript modules, a powerful feature that allows us to organize our code into reusable and maintainable units. We learned how to export and import modules, and we explored both CommonJS and ES modules. Modules help us write modular and scalable code, improving code organization and promoting code reuse. Tomorrow, we'll dive into asynchronous programming in JavaScript and explore concepts like callbacks, promises, and async/await. Keep up the great work, and see you in Day 10.

Day 10: Asynchronous Programming in JavaScript

Welcome to Day 10 of "Master JavaScript in 30 Days"!

Today, we'll explore asynchronous programming in JavaScript. Asynchronous programming allows us to handle tasks that may take some time to complete, such as fetching data from an API or reading from a file, without blocking the execution of other tasks. JavaScript provides several techniques for handling asynchronous operations effectively.

Topics Covered:

1. Introduction to Asynchronous Programming

2. Callback Functions

3. Promises

4. Async/Await

Introduction to Asynchronous Programming:

In synchronous programming, tasks are executed sequentially, and each task must complete before the next one begins. Asynchronous programming, on the other hand, allows multiple tasks to run concurrently, and the program can continue executing other tasks while waiting for certain operations to complete.

Asynchronous programming is crucial when dealing with time-consuming operations, such as network requests or file I/O, to prevent blocking the execution of other tasks and keep the application responsive.

Callback Functions:

Callback functions are a common way to handle asynchronous operations in JavaScript. A callback function is a function passed as an argument to another function and is invoked once the asynchronous operation completes. Here's an example:

```
function fetchData(callback) {

setTimeout(function() {
```

```
const data = "This is the fetched data";

callback(data);

}, 2000);

}

function process(data) {

console.log("Processing:", data);

}

fetchData(process);
```

In this example, the `fetchData` function simulates an asynchronous operation using `setTimeout`. Once the operation is complete, it invokes the provided callback function with the fetched data. The `process` function is passed as the callback and is executed with the fetched data.

Promises:

Promises provide a cleaner and more structured way to handle asynchronous operations. A promise represents the eventual completion (or failure) of an asynchronous operation and allows us to attach callback functions to handle the result. Here's an example:

```
function fetchData() {

return new Promise(function(resolve, reject) {

setTimeout(function() {

const data = "This is the fetched data";

resolve(data);

}, 2000);

});

}

function process(data) {
```

```
console.log("Processing:", data);

}

fetchData()

.then(process)

.catch(function(error) {

console.error("Error:", error);

});
```

In this example, the `fetchData` function returns a new Promise that wraps the asynchronous operation. The promise is resolved with the fetched data using the `resolve` function. The `process` function is then attached as a callback using the `then` method.

Promises provide additional benefits, such as chaining multiple asynchronous operations and handling errors using the `catch` method.

Async/Await:

Async/await is a modern syntax for handling asynchronous operations that builds upon promises. It provides a more synchronous and readable way to write asynchronous code. Here's an example:

```
function fetchData() {

return new Promise(function(resolve, reject) {

setTimeout(function() {

const data = "This is the fetched data";

resolve(data);

}, 2000);

});

}

async function process() {
```

```
try {

const data = await fetchData();

console.log("Processing:", data);

} catch (error) {

console.error("Error:", error);

}

}

process();
```

In this example, the `process` function is marked as `async`, indicating that it contains asynchronous operations. The `await` keyword is used to pause the execution of the function until the promise is resolved. Any errors are caught using a `try/catch` block.

Async/await provides a more linear and readable flow of asynchronous code, making it easier to understand and maintain.

That wraps up Day 10!

Today, we explored asynchronous programming in JavaScript. We learned about callback functions, promises, and the modern syntax of async/await. These techniques allow us to handle asynchronous tasks effectively and write more responsive and maintainable code. Tomorrow, we'll dive into JavaScript's built-in methods for manipulating arrays. Keep up the great work, and see you in Day 11.

Day 11: Array Manipulation in JavaScript

Welcome to Day 11 of "Master JavaScript in 30 Days"!

Today, we'll explore JavaScript's built-in methods for manipulating arrays. Arrays are a fundamental data structure in JavaScript, and having a solid understanding of array manipulation is essential for working with data effectively.

Topics Covered:

1. Introduction to Array Manipulation

2. Adding and Removing Elements

3. Modifying and Accessing Elements

4. Array Iteration and Transformation

Introduction to Array Manipulation:

Array manipulation involves performing various operations on arrays, such as adding and removing elements, modifying and accessing elements, and transforming arrays using iteration and other techniques. JavaScript provides a rich set of built-in methods to make array manipulation easier and more efficient.

Adding and Removing Elements:

JavaScript arrays come with methods to add and remove elements dynamically.

To add elements to an array, we can use the `push()` method to add elements to the end of the array, or the `unshift()` method to add elements to the beginning. Here's an example:

```
let fruits = ['apple', 'banana'];

fruits.push('orange');

console.log(fruits); // Outputs: ['apple', 'banana', 'orange']

fruits.unshift('grape');

console.log(fruits); // Outputs: ['grape', 'apple', 'banana', 'orange']
```

In this example, we add the elements 'orange' and 'grape' to the array using `push()` and `unshift()`, respectively.

To remove elements from an array, we can use the `pop()` method to remove the last element, or the `shift()` method to remove the first element. Here's an example:

let fruits = ['apple', 'banana', 'orange'];

fruits.pop();

console.log(fruits); // Outputs: ['apple', 'banana']

fruits.shift();

console.log(fruits); // Outputs: ['banana']

In this example, we remove the last element using `pop()`, and then remove the first element using `shift()`.

Modifying and Accessing Elements:

JavaScript arrays provide methods to modify and access specific elements within the array.

To modify an element at a specific index, we can simply assign a new value to that index. Here's an example:

let fruits = ['apple', 'banana', 'orange'];

fruits[1] = 'grape';

console.log(fruits); // Outputs: ['apple', 'grape', 'orange']

In this example, we change the element at index 1 to 'grape' by assigning a new value to that index.

To access elements in an array, we can use square brackets and specify the index. Here's an example:

let fruits = ['apple', 'banana', 'orange'];

console.log(fruits[0]); // Outputs: 'apple'

console.log(fruits[2]); // Outputs: 'orange'

In this example, we access the elements at index 0 and index 2 using square brackets.

Array Iteration and Transformation:

JavaScript provides several methods for iterating over and transforming arrays.

The `forEach()` method allows us to iterate over each element of an array and perform a specified action. Here's an example:

```
let numbers = [1, 2, 3, 4, 5];

numbers.forEach(function(number) {

console.log(number * 2);

});
```

In this example, we use `forEach()` to iterate over each element in the `numbers` array and multiply it by 2.

The `map()` method creates a new array by applying a transformation function to each element of the original array. Here's an example:

```
let numbers = [1, 2, 3, 4, 5];

let doubledNumbers = numbers.map(function(number) {

return number * 2;

});

console.log(doubledNumbers); // Outputs: [2, 4, 6, 8, 10]
```

In this example, we use `map()` to create a new array, `doubledNumbers`, by multiplying each element of the `numbers` array by 2.

Other commonly used array methods for transformation include `filter()`, `reduce()`, and `sort()`, among others.

That wraps up Day 11!

Today, we explored array manipulation in JavaScript. We learned how to add and remove elements, modify and access elements, and perform iteration and transformation on arrays. Arrays are a powerful tool for working with collections of data, and mastering array manipulation techniques will greatly enhance your JavaScript skills. Tomorrow, we'll dive into working with objects in JavaScript. Keep up the great work, and see you in Day 12.

Day 12: Working with Objects

Welcome to Day 12 of "Master JavaScript in 30 Days"!

Today, we'll explore working with objects in JavaScript. Objects are a fundamental part of the language and allow us to represent and manipulate complex data structures. Understanding how to create, access, modify, and interact with objects is essential for building robust JavaScript applications.

Topics Covered:

1. Introduction to Objects

2. Creating Objects

3. Accessing and Modifying Object Properties

4. Object Methods and Prototypes

Introduction to Objects:

In JavaScript, objects are a collection of key-value pairs and represent entities with properties and behaviors. Objects can be used to model real-world objects, such as a person or a car, or to encapsulate related data and functionality.

Creating Objects:

There are multiple ways to create objects in JavaScript.

1. Object Literal Notation:

The simplest way to create an object is using object literal notation, denoted by curly braces `{}`. Here's an example:

```
let person = {

name: 'John Doe',

age: 30,

occupation: 'Developer'

};
```

In this example, we create an object `person` with properties such as `name`, `age`, and `occupation`, each assigned a value.

2. Constructor Function:

Constructor functions are used to create multiple objects with similar properties and behaviors. Here's an example:

```
function Person(name, age, occupation) {

this.name = name;

this.age = age;

this.occupation = occupation;

}

let person = new Person('John Doe', 30, 'Developer');
```

In this example, we define a constructor function `Person` that takes parameters `name`, `age`, and `occupation`. We use the `new` keyword to create a new instance of the `Person` object.

Accessing and Modifying Object Properties:

We can access and modify object properties using dot notation (`object.property`) or bracket notation (`object['property']`). Here's an example:

```
let person = {

name: 'John Doe',

age: 30,

occupation: 'Developer'

};

console.log(person.name); // Outputs: 'John Doe'

person.age = 35;

console.log(person['age']); // Outputs: 35
```

In this example, we access the `name` property using dot notation and modify the `age` property using bracket notation.

Object Methods and Prototypes:

Objects can also have methods, which are functions defined as object properties. Methods allow objects to perform actions and encapsulate behaviors. Here's an example:

```
let person = {

name: 'John Doe',

age: 30,

occupation: 'Developer',

greet: function() {

console.log('Hello, my name is ' + this.name);

}

};

person.greet(); // Outputs: 'Hello, my name is John Doe'
```

In this example, the `person` object has a method `greet()` that logs a greeting message using the object's `name` property.

JavaScript also supports prototypal inheritance, where objects can inherit properties and methods from other objects. This allows for code reuse and object relationships. However, a detailed exploration of prototypes and inheritance is beyond the scope of this lesson.

That wraps up Day 12!

Today, we explored working with objects in JavaScript. We learned how to create objects using object literal notation and constructor functions, access and modify object properties, and define object methods. Objects provide a powerful way to organize and manipulate data in JavaScript. Tomorrow, we'll dive into error handling and debugging techniques in JavaScript. Keep up the great work, and see you in Day 13.

Day 13: Error Handling and Debugging

Welcome to Day 13 of "Master JavaScript in 30 Days"!

Today, we'll explore error handling and debugging techniques in JavaScript. As you write more complex JavaScript code, it's essential to understand how to handle errors effectively and debug your code to identify and fix issues.

Topics Covered:

1. Introduction to Error Handling

2. Types of Errors

3. Error Handling Techniques

4. Debugging Techniques

Introduction to Error Handling:

Errors are a common part of programming, and JavaScript provides mechanisms to handle them gracefully. Error handling involves detecting and managing errors that occur during the execution of your code to prevent crashes and provide meaningful feedback to users.

Types of Errors:

JavaScript categorizes errors into different types based on their nature. Some common error types include:

1. Syntax Errors: These occur when the JavaScript parser encounters code that violates the language's syntax rules.

2. Runtime Errors: These occur during the execution of the code when unexpected conditions or actions are encountered, such as accessing undefined variables or calling non-existent functions.

3. Logic Errors: These occur when the code does not produce the expected output due to flaws in the program's logic or algorithm.

Error Handling Techniques:

JavaScript provides several techniques to handle errors and prevent them from causing your application to crash.

1. Try-Catch Statement:

The `try-catch` statement allows you to catch and handle specific errors within a block of code. Here's an example:

```
try {

// Code that may throw an error

} catch (error) {

// Code to handle the error

}
```

In this example, the code within the `try` block is executed. If an error occurs, the `catch` block is executed, and the `error` parameter contains information about the error.

2. Throwing Custom Errors:

You can also throw custom errors using the `throw` statement. This allows you to create specific error conditions and handle them accordingly. Here's an example:

```
function divide(a, b) {

if (b === 0) {

throw new Error('Division by zero is not allowed');

}

return a / b;

}

try {

console.log(divide(10, 0));

} catch (error) {
```

```
console.error(error.message);

}
```

In this example, the `divide` function throws a custom `Error` object if the divisor `b` is zero. The `try-catch` statement catches the error and logs its message.

Debugging Techniques:

Debugging is the process of identifying and fixing errors in your code. JavaScript provides several tools and techniques to help you debug your code effectively.

1. Logging:

Using `console.log()` statements at different points in your code can help you understand the flow and values of variables. You can log messages and variable values to the browser's console for inspection.

2. Debugging Tools:

Most modern web browsers come with built-in developer tools that include powerful debugging capabilities. These tools allow you to set breakpoints, step through code execution, inspect variables, and track the flow of your code.

3. Debugging Statements:

JavaScript provides the `debugger` statement, which triggers a breakpoint in your code when encountered. You can place the `debugger` statement at specific locations to pause execution and inspect the state of your program.

That wraps up Day 13!

Today, we explored error handling and debugging techniques in JavaScript. We learned about different error types, error handling with `try-catch` statements, throwing custom errors, and various debugging techniques. Effective error handling and debugging skills are crucial for maintaining code quality and resolving issues in your JavaScript applications. Tomorrow, we'll dive into working with JSON data in JavaScript. Keep up the great work, and see you in Day 14.

Day 14: Working with JSON Data

Welcome to Day 14 of "Master JavaScript in 30 Days"!

Today, we'll explore working with JSON (JavaScript Object Notation) data in JavaScript. JSON is a widely used data format for storing and transmitting structured data, and JavaScript provides built-in methods to work with JSON effectively.

Topics Covered:

1. Introduction to JSON

2. JSON Syntax

3. Converting Between JSON and JavaScript Objects

4. Parsing and Stringifying JSON

Introduction to JSON:

JSON (JavaScript Object Notation) is a lightweight data interchange format that is easy for humans to read and write and easy for machines to parse and generate. It is based on key-value pairs and supports various data types, including strings, numbers, booleans, arrays, and objects. JSON is commonly used for data storage, configuration files, and data exchange between client and server applications.

JSON Syntax:

JSON syntax is inspired by JavaScript object and array literals but with some differences. Here are a few key points to remember:

1. Data is represented in key-value pairs enclosed in curly braces `{}`.

2. Keys must be strings enclosed in double quotes.

3. Values can be strings, numbers, booleans, arrays, objects, or null.

4. Multiple key-value pairs are separated by commas.

Here's an example of a simple JSON object:

{

```
"name": "John Doe",

"age": 30,

"occupation": "Developer"

}
```

Converting Between JSON and JavaScript Objects:

JavaScript provides methods to convert between JSON and JavaScript objects seamlessly.

1. Converting JavaScript Objects to JSON:

The `JSON.stringify()` method converts a JavaScript object to a JSON string. Here's an example:

```
let person = {

name: "John Doe",

age: 30,

occupation: "Developer"

};

let json = JSON.stringify(person);

console.log(json);
```

In this example, the `person` object is converted to a JSON string using `JSON.stringify()`.

2. Converting JSON to JavaScript Objects:

The `JSON.parse()` method converts a JSON string to a JavaScript object. Here's an example:

```
let json = '{"name":"John Doe","age":30,"occupation":"Developer"}';

let person = JSON.parse(json);

console.log(person);
```

In this example, the `json` string is converted to a JavaScript object using `JSON.parse()`.

Parsing and Stringifying JSON:

JavaScript provides methods to parse and stringify JSON data effectively.

1. Parsing JSON:

The `JSON.parse()` method parses a JSON string and returns a JavaScript object. Here's an example:

```javascript
let json = '{"name":"John Doe","age":30,"occupation":"Developer"}';

let person = JSON.parse(json);

console.log(person.name); // Outputs: "John Doe"
```

In this example, we parse the `json` string and access the `name` property of the resulting JavaScript object.

2. Stringifying JavaScript Objects:

The `JSON.stringify()` method converts a JavaScript object to a JSON string. Here's an example:

```javascript
let person = {

name: "John Doe",

age: 30,

occupation: "Developer"

};

let json = JSON.stringify(person);

console.log(json); // Outputs: '{"name":"John Doe","age":30,"occupation":"Developer"}'
```

In this example, we convert the `person` object to a JSON string using `JSON.stringify()`.

That wraps up Day 14!

Today, we explored working with JSON data in JavaScript. We learned about JSON syntax, converting between JSON and JavaScript objects using `JSON.stringify()` and `JSON.parse()`, and the importance of parsing and stringifying JSON data. JSON is a widely used format for data storage and exchange, and mastering its usage is essential for working with APIs and managing structured data in

JavaScript. Tomorrow, we'll dive into asynchronous programming and callbacks in JavaScript. Keep up the great work, and see you in Day 15.

Day 15: Asynchronous Programming and Callbacks

Welcome to Day 15 of "Master JavaScript in 30 Days"!

Today, we'll explore asynchronous programming and callbacks in JavaScript. Asynchronous programming allows us to execute code concurrently, handle time-consuming tasks efficiently, and maintain the responsiveness of our applications. Callbacks are a fundamental part of asynchronous programming in JavaScript.

Topics Covered:

1. Introduction to Asynchronous Programming

2. Callback Functions

3. Handling Asynchronous Operations with Callbacks

4. Callback Hell and Solutions

Introduction to Asynchronous Programming:

JavaScript is a single-threaded language, meaning it can only execute one task at a time. However, it supports asynchronous programming to handle time-consuming tasks, such as network requests, file operations, or animations, without blocking the execution of other code.

Callback Functions:

A callback function is a function that is passed as an argument to another function and is executed later, often after completing an asynchronous operation. Callbacks allow us to define what should happen when an asynchronous task is finished.

function asyncOperation(callback) {

// Simulating an asynchronous task

setTimeout(function() {

// Task completed

callback();

```
}, 2000);

}

function callbackFunction() {

console.log("Async operation completed!");

}

asyncOperation(callbackFunction);
```

In this example, `asyncOperation` simulates an asynchronous task using `setTimeout`. It accepts a `callback` function as an argument and executes it after 2 seconds.

Handling Asynchronous Operations with Callbacks:

When working with asynchronous operations, we typically provide a callback function to handle the result or any errors once the operation is complete. Here's an example using the `fetch` API to make an HTTP request:

```
function fetchData(url, callback) {

fetch(url)

.then(response => response.json())

.then(data => callback(null, data))

.catch(error => callback(error, null));

}

function handleData(error, data) {

if (error) {

console.error("An error occurred:", error);

} else {

console.log("Data received:", data);
```

```
}

}
```

fetchData("https://api.example.com/data", handleData);

In this example, the `fetchData` function makes an HTTP request to a specified URL. It calls the `callback` function with the error as the first argument and the data as the second argument, depending on the success or failure of the request.

Callback Hell and Solutions:

Asynchronous programming with callbacks can lead to a situation called "callback hell" or "pyramid of doom" when dealing with multiple nested asynchronous operations. This can make code hard to read and maintain. To mitigate this, there are several solutions:

1. Use Named Functions: Extract callback functions into named functions to improve readability and separate concerns.

2. Use Promises: Promises provide a cleaner and more structured way to handle asynchronous operations. They allow you to chain multiple operations and handle success and error cases separately.

3. Use Async/Await: The `async/await` syntax simplifies asynchronous programming further by allowing you to write asynchronous code that looks like synchronous code, making it easier to understand and maintain.

That wraps up Day 15!

Today, we explored asynchronous programming and callbacks in JavaScript. We learned how to use callbacks to handle asynchronous operations, how to mitigate callback hell, and the alternatives like Promises and Async/Await. Asynchronous programming is crucial for building responsive and efficient JavaScript applications. Tomorrow, we'll dive into working with modules in JavaScript. Keep up the great work, and see you in Day 16.

Day 16: Working with Modules

Welcome to Day 16 of "Master JavaScript in 30 Days"!

Today, we'll explore working with modules in JavaScript. Modules allow us to organize and encapsulate our code, making it more modular, reusable, and maintainable. JavaScript provides built-in support for modules through the ES Modules (ESM) syntax.

Topics Covered:

1. Introduction to Modules

2. Creating and Exporting Modules

3. Importing Modules

4. Default Exports and Named Exports

Introduction to Modules:

Modules are self-contained units of code that encapsulate functionality, variables, and data. They help us break down our code into smaller, manageable pieces, and allow for better code organization, reusability, and separation of concerns.

Creating and Exporting Modules:

In JavaScript, a module can be any file containing JavaScript code. To create a module, we use the ES Modules (ESM) syntax, which consists of the `export` keyword to export functionality from a module.

Let's say we have a file named `utils.js` with the following code:

```
// utils.js

export function square(x) {

return x * x;

}

export const PI = 3.14159;
```

In this example, we have a module that exports a function `square()` and a constant `PI` using the `export` keyword.

Importing Modules:

To use functionality from a module, we need to import it into another module. The `import` keyword is used to import functionality from other modules.

Let's say we have another file named `main.js` where we want to use the `square()` function and the `PI` constant from the `utils.js` module:

```
// main.js

import { square, PI } from './utils.js';

console.log(square(5)); // Outputs: 25

console.log(PI); // Outputs: 3.14159
```

In this example, we import the `square()` function and the `PI` constant from the `utils.js` module using the `import` keyword and provide the module path.

Default Exports and Named Exports:

In addition to named exports, JavaScript modules also support default exports. A default export represents the main functionality or value of a module.

Let's modify our `utils.js` module to include a default export:

```
// utils.js

export function square(x) {

return x * x;

}

export const PI = 3.14159;

export default function greet(name) {

console.log(`Hello, ${name}!`);
```

```
}
```

In this example, we added a default export `greet()` to the `utils.js` module.

To import the default export, we can use a different syntax:

```
// main.js

import greet from './utils.js';

greet('John'); // Outputs: Hello, John!
```

In this example, we import the default export `greet()` from the `utils.js` module without using curly braces.

That wraps up Day 16!

Today, we explored working with modules in JavaScript. We learned how to create and export modules using the `export` keyword, import functionality from modules using the `import` keyword, and differentiate between default exports and named exports. Modules are a powerful feature in JavaScript that help us write modular and reusable code. Tomorrow, we'll dive into working with Promises in JavaScript. Keep up the great work, and see you in Day 17.

Day 17: Promises in JavaScript

Welcome to Day 17 of "Master JavaScript in 30 Days"!

Today, we'll explore Promises in JavaScript. Promises are a powerful tool for handling asynchronous operations and managing the flow of asynchronous code. They provide a more structured and readable way to work with asynchronous tasks.

Topics Covered:

1. Introduction to Promises

2. Creating a Promise

3. Handling Promise States: Pending, Fulfilled, and Rejected

4. Chaining Promises with `then()` and `catch()`

5. Handling Multiple Promises with `Promise.all()`

Introduction to Promises:

Promises are objects that represent the eventual completion or failure of an asynchronous operation and allow us to handle the result or errors once the operation is complete. Promises simplify asynchronous programming and provide a more structured approach compared to traditional callbacks.

Creating a Promise:

To create a Promise, we use the `Promise` constructor and pass a function with two parameters: `resolve` and `reject`. Inside this function, we perform our asynchronous operation and call `resolve` when it is successful or `reject` when it encounters an error.

Here's an example that demonstrates the basic structure of a Promise:

const promise = new Promise((resolve, reject) => {

// Asynchronous operation

// If successful:

resolve("Operation completed successfully!");

```
// If error occurs:

reject("An error occurred!");

});
```

In this example, we create a Promise that represents an asynchronous operation. If the operation is successful, we call `resolve` with a value. If an error occurs, we call `reject` with an error message.

Handling Promise States: Pending, Fulfilled, and Rejected:

Promises have three states:

1. Pending: The initial state when the Promise is created and the asynchronous operation is still ongoing.

2. Fulfilled: The state when the Promise is resolved successfully with a value.

3. Rejected: The state when the Promise encounters an error and is rejected with a reason.

Once a Promise is settled (fulfilled or rejected), its state cannot be changed.

Chaining Promises with `then()` and `catch()`:

Promises can be chained together using the `then()` method to handle the resolved value and the `catch()` method to handle any errors. The `then()` method takes a callback function that is executed when the Promise is fulfilled, and the `catch()` method takes a callback function that is executed when the Promise is rejected.

Here's an example that demonstrates Promise chaining:

```
asyncOperation()

.then(result => {

// Handle fulfilled state

console.log("Operation succeeded:", result);

return anotherAsyncOperation();

})
```

```
.then(data => {

// Handle fulfilled state of the second Promise

console.log("Another operation succeeded:", data);

})

.catch(error => {

// Handle any errors in the chain

console.error("An error occurred:", error);

});
```

In this example, we chain two Promises together using `then()`. If any Promise in the chain is rejected, the `catch()` block will be executed.

Handling Multiple Promises with `Promise.all()`:

The `Promise.all()` method allows us to handle multiple Promises concurrently and wait for all of them to fulfill or reject. It takes an array of Promises as input and returns a new Promise that resolves to an array of resolved values or rejects with the reason of the first rejected Promise.

Here's an example that demonstrates the usage of `Promise.all()`:

```
const promise1 = someAsyncOperation();

const promise2 = anotherAsyncOperation();

const promise3 = yetAnotherAsyncOperation();

Promise.all([promise1, promise

2, promise3])

.then(results => {

// Handle the resolved values of all Promises

console.log("All operations completed:", results);
```

```
})

.catch(error => {

// Handle any error that occurred

console.error("An error occurred:", error);

});
```

In this example, we create three Promises and pass them to `Promise.all()`. The `then()` block is executed when all Promises are fulfilled, and the `catch()` block is executed if any of the Promises are rejected.

That wraps up Day 17!

Today, we explored Promises in JavaScript. We learned how to create Promises, handle their states, chain Promises using `then()` and `catch()`, and handle multiple Promises concurrently using `Promise.all()`. Promises provide a more structured and readable way to work with asynchronous code. Tomorrow, we'll dive into working with async/await in JavaScript. Keep up the great work, and see you in Day 18.

Day 18: Async/Await in JavaScript

Welcome to Day 18 of "Master JavaScript in 30 Days"!

Today, we'll explore async/await, a modern approach to handling asynchronous code in JavaScript. Async/await provides a more concise and synchronous-looking syntax for working with Promises, making asynchronous programming easier to read and write.

Topics Covered:

1. Introduction to Async/Await

2. The `async` Keyword

3. The `await` Keyword

4. Error Handling with Try/Catch

5. Converting Callbacks to Async/Await

Introduction to Async/Await:

Async/await is a syntax introduced in ECMAScript 2017 (ES8) that simplifies working with Promises and makes asynchronous code look more like synchronous code. It provides a cleaner and more intuitive way to write and handle asynchronous operations.

The `async` Keyword:

To define an asynchronous function, we use the `async` keyword before the function declaration. An async function always returns a Promise, which resolves to the value returned by the function or rejects with an error thrown from within the function.

Here's an example that demonstrates the usage of the `async` keyword:

```
async function fetchData() {

// Asynchronous operation

return await someAsyncOperation();

}
```

In this example, the `fetchData` function is defined as an async function. It performs an asynchronous operation using `await` and returns a Promise.

The `await` Keyword:

The `await` keyword can only be used inside an async function. It pauses the execution of the function until the Promise is fulfilled or rejected. It allows us to write asynchronous code that looks like synchronous code.

Here's an example that demonstrates the usage of the `await` keyword:

async function fetchData() {

try {

const data = await someAsyncOperation();

console.log("Data received:", data);

} catch (error) {

console.error("An error occurred:", error);

}

}

In this example, the `await` keyword is used to wait for the `someAsyncOperation` Promise to resolve. The code inside the `try` block is executed when the Promise is fulfilled, and any errors are caught in the `catch` block.

Error Handling with Try/Catch:

When working with async/await, error handling can be done using the familiar `try/catch` block. The `try` block contains the code that may throw an error, and the `catch` block handles the error if one occurs.

Converting Callbacks to Async/Await:

Async/await can also be used to convert callback-based functions into Promise-based functions. By wrapping a callback function with a Promise, we can use async/await to handle the result or error.

Here's an example that demonstrates converting a callback function to async/await:

```
function fetchData(callback) {

someAsyncOperation((error, data) => {

if (error) {

callback(error, null);

} else {

callback(null, data);

}

});

}

// Converted to async/await

async function fetchData() {

try {

const data = await new Promise((resolve, reject) => {

someAsyncOperation((error, data) => {

if (error) {

reject(error);

} else {

resolve(data);

}

});

});
```

```
console.log("Data received:", data);

} catch (error) {

console.error("An error occurred:", error);

}

}
```

In this example, the `fetchData` function is converted to use async/await by wrapping the callback-based `someAsyncOperation` function with a Promise.

That wraps up Day 18!

Today, we explored async/await, a modern approach to handling asynchronous code in JavaScript. We learned how to define async functions using the `async` keyword, use the `await` keyword to pause execution until a Promise is resolved, handle errors with `try/catch`, and convert callback functions to async/await. Async/await provides a cleaner and more synchronous-looking syntax for asynchronous programming. Tomorrow, we'll delve into working with JavaScript's Object-Oriented Programming (OOP) concepts. Keep up the great work, and see you in Day 19.

Day 19: Object-Oriented Programming

Welcome to Day 19 of "Master JavaScript in 30 Days"!

Today, we'll dive into Object-Oriented Programming (OOP) concepts in JavaScript. OOP is a popular paradigm that allows us to structure our code around objects and their interactions. JavaScript, being a versatile language, supports OOP features.

Topics Covered:

1. Introduction to Object-Oriented Programming (OOP)

2. Objects and Classes in JavaScript

3. Creating Objects with Constructor Functions

4. The Prototype Chain

5. Inheritance and Prototypes

Introduction to Object-Oriented Programming (OOP):

Object-Oriented Programming is a programming paradigm that focuses on creating objects that encapsulate data and behavior. OOP provides concepts such as encapsulation, inheritance, and polymorphism, which help in writing modular and reusable code.

Objects and Classes in JavaScript:

In JavaScript, objects are key-value pairs that can hold data and behavior. They can be created using object literals or constructor functions. Additionally, JavaScript also introduced the `class` syntax in ECMAScript 2015 (ES6), which provides a more standardized way to define classes.

Here's an example of creating an object using object literals:

```
const person = {

name: "John",

age: 30,

greet() {
```

```
console.log(`Hello, my name is ${this.name} and I'm ${this.age} years old.`);

},

};
```

In this example, we define an object `person` with properties `name` and `age`, as well as a method `greet()`.

Creating Objects with Constructor Functions:

Constructor functions are used to create objects with a shared structure and behavior. They are invoked using the `new` keyword and allow us to create multiple instances of an object.

Here's an example of creating objects using a constructor function:

```
function Person(name, age) {

this.name = name;

this.age = age;

this.greet = function() {

console.log(`Hello, my name is ${this.name} and I'm ${this.age} years old.`);

};

}

const person1 = new Person("John", 30);

const person2 = new Person("Jane", 25);
```

In this example, we define a constructor function `Person` that initializes properties `name` and `age`, as well as a method `greet()`. We create two instances of the `Person` object using the `new` keyword.

The Prototype Chain:

In JavaScript, objects have a special property called `prototype`. The `prototype` property allows objects to inherit properties and methods from other objects. When a property or method is accessed on an object, JavaScript looks for it in the object itself, and if not found, it looks up the prototype chain.

Here's an example that demonstrates the prototype chain:

```javascript
function Animal(name) {

this.name = name;

}

Animal.prototype.speak = function() {

console.log(`${this.name} makes a sound.`);

};

function Dog(name) {

Animal.call(this, name);

}

Dog.prototype = Object.create(Animal.prototype);

Dog.prototype.constructor = Dog;

Dog.prototype.speak = function() {

console.log(`${this.name} barks.`);

};

const dog = new Dog("Max");

dog.speak(); // Outputs: "Max barks."
```

In this example, we have an `Animal` constructor function with a `speak()` method defined on its prototype. We create a `Dog` constructor function that inherits from `Animal` using `Object.create()`. The `Dog` constructor overrides the `speak()` method.

Inheritance and Prototypes:

JavaScript implements inheritance using prototypes. By setting the prototype of a child object to the prototype of a parent object, we can establish an inheritance relationship. The child object can then access properties and methods defined in the parent object's prototype.

That wraps up Day 19!

Today, we explored Object-Oriented Programming (OOP) concepts in JavaScript. We learned about objects and classes, creating objects with constructor functions, the prototype chain, and inheritance using prototypes. OOP allows us to create reusable and modular code structures. Tomorrow, we'll dive into working with modules in JavaScript. Keep up the great work, and see you in Day 20.

Day 20: Modules in JavaScript

Welcome to Day 20 of "Master JavaScript in 30 Days"!

Today, we'll explore modules in JavaScript. Modules allow us to organize and separate our code into reusable and self-contained units. JavaScript modules provide a way to encapsulate code and control the visibility of variables and functions.

Topics Covered:

1. Introduction to Modules

2. Exporting from Modules

3. Importing Modules

4. Default Exports and Named Exports

5. Module Bundlers and Transpilers

Introduction to Modules:

Modules in JavaScript allow us to split our code into separate files, making it easier to manage and maintain. Each module encapsulates its own variables, functions, or classes and can be imported and used in other modules.

Exporting from Modules:

To make variables, functions, or classes available outside a module, we need to export them. In JavaScript, we have two types of exports: default exports and named exports.

Here's an example of exporting a function as a default export:

```
// math.js module

export default function add(a, b) {

return a + b;

}
```

In this example, we export the `add` function as a default export using the `export default` syntax.

Here's an example of exporting multiple functions as named exports:

```
// math.js module

export function add(a, b) {

return a + b;

}

export function subtract(a, b) {

return a - b;

}
```

In this example, we export the `add` and `subtract` functions as named exports.

Importing Modules:

To use code from a module in another module, we need to import it. In JavaScript, we use the `import` keyword to import variables, functions, or classes from a module.

Here's an example of importing a default export:

```
// app.js module

import add from "./math.js";

console.log(add(2, 3)); // Outputs: 5
```

In this example, we import the default export from the `math.js` module using the `import` statement. We can then use the imported function in our code.

Here's an example of importing named exports:

```
// app.js module

import { add, subtract } from "./math.js";

console.log(add(2, 3)); // Outputs: 5

console.log(subtract(5, 2)); // Outputs: 3
```

In this example, we import the `add` and `subtract` functions as named exports from the `math.js` module. We can use these imported functions in our code.

Default Exports and Named Exports:

Default exports allow us to export a single value from a module, while named exports allow us to export multiple values.

When importing a default export, we can choose any name we want. For named exports, we need to use the exact names specified in the export statement.

Here's an example that combines default and named exports:

// math.js module

export default function add(a, b) {

return a + b;

}

export function subtract(a, b) {

return a - b;

}

// app.js module

import myAdd, { subtract } from "./math.js";

console.log(myAdd(2, 3)); // Outputs: 5

console.log(subtract(5, 2)); // Outputs: 3

In this example, we import the default export as `myAdd` and the named export `subtract` from the `math.js` module.

Module Bundlers and Transpilers:

JavaScript modules are natively supported in modern browsers and environments. However, to ensure compatibility with older browsers and to leverage advanced features, we often use module bundlers like webpack or transpilers like Babel.

Module bundlers combine multiple modules into a single file, optimizing the code for production. Transpilers, on the other hand, convert modern JavaScript syntax into an older version of JavaScript that is supported by more browsers.

That wraps up Day 20!

Today, we explored modules in JavaScript. We learned about exporting from modules, importing modules, default exports, named exports, and the role of module bundlers and transpilers. Modules provide a clean and organized way to structure our code and promote reusability. Tomorrow, we'll dive into working with JavaScript's built-in Date and Time objects. Keep up the great work, and see you in Day 21.

Day 21: Date and Time in JavaScript

Welcome to Day 21 of "Master JavaScript in 30 Days"!

Today, we'll explore Date and Time in JavaScript. Working with dates and times is a common task in many applications, and JavaScript provides built-in objects and methods to handle them effectively.

Topics Covered:

1. Introduction to Date and Time in JavaScript

2. Creating Date Objects

3. Working with Dates and Times

4. Formatting Dates and Times

5. Performing Date Calculations

Introduction to Date and Time in JavaScript:

In JavaScript, the `Date` object is used to work with dates and times. It provides methods for creating, manipulating, and formatting dates and times. The `Date` object represents a specific moment in time.

Creating Date Objects:

To create a `Date` object, we can use the `new` keyword followed by the `Date()` constructor. The `Date` constructor can take various arguments such as year, month, day, hour, minute, second, and millisecond.

Here's an example of creating a `Date` object:

const now = new Date();

console.log(now); // Outputs the current date and time

In this example, we create a `Date` object called `now`, which represents the current date and time.

Working with Dates and Times:

The `Date` object provides various methods for working with dates and times. Some commonly used methods are:

- `getFullYear()`: Returns the year (4 digits).

- `getMonth()`: Returns the month (0-11).

- `getDate()`: Returns the day of the month (1-31).

- `getHours()`: Returns the hour (0-23).

- `getMinutes()`: Returns the minutes (0-59).

- `getSeconds()`: Returns the seconds (0-59).

- `getMilliseconds()`: Returns the milliseconds (0-999).

Here's an example that demonstrates working with date and time methods:

```
const now = new Date();

console.log(now.getFullYear()); // Outputs the current year

console.log(now.getMonth()); // Outputs the current month

console.log(now.getDate()); // Outputs the current day

console.log(now.getHours()); // Outputs the current hour

console.log(now.getMinutes()); // Outputs the current minutes

console.log(now.getSeconds()); // Outputs the current seconds

console.log(now.getMilliseconds()); // Outputs the current milliseconds
```

Formatting Dates and Times:

The `Date` object also provides methods to format dates and times as strings. Some commonly used methods are:

- `toString()`: Returns the date and time as a string.

- `toDateString()`: Returns the date as a string (without the time).

- `toLocaleString()`: Returns a localized date and time string.

Here's an example that demonstrates formatting date and time:

```
const now = new Date();
```

```
console.log(now.toString()); // Outputs the date and time as a string
```

```
console.log(now.toDateString()); // Outputs the date as a string
```

```
console.log(now.toLocaleString()); // Outputs a localized date and time string
```

Performing Date Calculations:

The `Date` object allows us to perform various calculations and manipulations on dates. We can set specific parts of a date, add or subtract days, months, or years, and compare dates using comparison operators.

Here's an example that demonstrates date calculations:

```
const now = new Date();
```

```
const tomorrow = new Date();
```

```
tomorrow.setDate(now.getDate() + 1); // Adds 1 day to the current date
```

```
console.log(now < tomorrow); // Outputs true (now is before tomorrow)
```

In this example, we create a `tomorrow` `Date` object by adding one day to the current date using the `setDate()` method. We then compare the two dates using the `<` operator.

That wraps up Day 21!

Today, we explored Date and Time in JavaScript. We learned how to create `Date` objects, work with dates and times using various methods, format dates and times as strings, and perform date calculations. Dates and times are an essential part of many applications, and JavaScript provides powerful tools to handle them. Tomorrow, we'll dive into working with JavaScript's built-in Regular Expressions. Keep up the great work, and see you in Day 22.

Day 22: Regular Expressions

Welcome to Day 22 of "Master JavaScript in 30 Days"!

Today, we'll explore Regular Expressions in JavaScript. Regular Expressions, often abbreviated as regex, provide a powerful and flexible way to search, match, and manipulate text patterns. They are widely used for tasks such as validation, searching, and replacing strings.

Topics Covered:

1. Introduction to Regular Expressions

2. Creating Regular Expressions

3. Matching Patterns

4. Modifiers and Flags

5. Replacing and Extracting Patterns

Introduction to Regular Expressions:

A Regular Expression is a sequence of characters that forms a search pattern. It can be used to match and manipulate strings based on certain rules or patterns. Regular Expressions provide a concise and powerful way to work with text patterns.

Creating Regular Expressions:

In JavaScript, Regular Expressions can be created using the `RegExp` object or by using literal notation with forward slashes (`/`). Literal notation is commonly used as it provides a more concise syntax.

Here's an example of creating a Regular Expression using literal notation:

const regex = /pattern/;

In this example, we create a Regular Expression that matches the pattern "pattern".

Matching Patterns:

Regular Expressions provide methods to match patterns in strings. Some commonly used methods are:

- `test()`: Tests if a pattern is found in a string and returns `true` or `false`.

- `exec()`: Searches for a pattern in a string and returns an array containing the matched results.

Here's an example that demonstrates pattern matching using Regular Expressions:

const str = "Hello, World!";

const regex = /o/;

console.log(regex.test(str)); // Outputs: true

console.log(regex.exec(str)); // Outputs: ["o"]

In this example, we test if the pattern "o" is found in the string using the `test()` method. We also use the `exec()` method to search for the pattern and retrieve the matched result.

Modifiers and Flags:

Regular Expressions can have modifiers or flags that affect how the pattern is matched. Some commonly used modifiers are:

- `i`: Case-insensitive matching.

- `g`: Global matching (find all matches rather than stopping at the first match).

- `m`: Multiline matching.

Modifiers can be added to a Regular Expression by appending them after the closing slash (`/`).

Here's an example that demonstrates the use of modifiers:

const str = "Hello, World!";

const regex = /o/gi;

console.log(str.match(regex)); // Outputs: ["o", "o"]

In this example, we use the `g` modifier to perform a global match and the `i` modifier to perform a case-insensitive match. The `match()` method returns an array containing all the matched results.

Replacing and Extracting Patterns:

Regular Expressions can also be used to replace or extract patterns in strings. JavaScript provides the `replace()` method to replace patterns and the `match()` method to extract patterns.

Here's an example that demonstrates replacing and extracting patterns:

const str = "Hello, World!";

const regex = /o/g;

console.log(str.replace(regex, "a")); // Outputs: "Hella, Warld!"

console.log(str.match(regex)); // Outputs: ["o", "o"]

In this example, we use the `replace()` method to replace all occurrences of the pattern "o" with the letter "a". We use the `match()` method to extract all occurrences of the pattern "o".

That wraps up Day 22!

Today, we explored Regular Expressions in JavaScript. We learned how to create Regular Expressions using literal notation, match patterns in strings using methods like `test()` and `exec()`, use modifiers and flags for advanced matching, and replace or extract patterns using methods like `replace()` and `match()`. Regular Expressions are a powerful tool for working with text patterns in JavaScript. Tomorrow, we'll dive into error handling and exception handling in JavaScript. Keep up the great work, and see you in Day 23.

Day 23: Error Handling in JavaScript

Welcome to Day 23 of "Master JavaScript in 30 Days"!

Today, we'll explore error handling and exception handling in JavaScript. Errors are a common occurrence in programming, and understanding how to handle them effectively is essential for writing robust and reliable code.

Topics Covered:

1. Introduction to Error Handling

2. Types of Errors

3. try...catch Statement

4. Throwing Custom Errors

5. Error Handling Best Practices

Introduction to Error Handling:

Error handling is the process of identifying, catching, and handling errors that occur during the execution of a program. JavaScript provides a built-in mechanism to handle errors using the `try...catch` statement. By handling errors properly, we can gracefully recover from errors and prevent our programs from crashing.

Types of Errors:

JavaScript has several types of errors, including:

- SyntaxError: Occurs when there is a syntax error in the code.

- ReferenceError: Occurs when referencing an undefined variable or object.

- TypeError: Occurs when performing an operation on an incompatible type.

- RangeError: Occurs when using a value outside the range of acceptable values.

- Custom Errors: Errors that we define ourselves to handle specific situations.

try...catch Statement:

The `try...catch` statement is used to catch and handle errors in JavaScript. The `try` block contains the code that may potentially throw an error, while the `catch` block is used to handle the error if it occurs.

Here's an example of using the `try...catch` statement:

```
try {

// Code that may throw an error

} catch (error) {

// Code to handle the error

}
```

In this example, we place the code that may throw an error inside the `try` block. If an error occurs, it is caught by the `catch` block, and we can handle it accordingly.

Throwing Custom Errors:

In addition to handling built-in errors, we can also throw custom errors to handle specific situations in our code. Custom errors can provide additional information and context about the error, making it easier to debug and handle.

Here's an example of throwing a custom error:

```
try {

throw new Error("Custom Error Message");

} catch (error) {

console.log(error.message); // Outputs: "Custom Error Message"

}
```

In this example, we use the `throw` keyword to throw a new `Error` object with a custom error message. The error is caught by the `catch` block, and we can access the error message using the `message` property.

Error Handling Best Practices:

When handling errors in JavaScript, consider the following best practices:

- Use specific error types: Instead of relying only on the generic `Error` type, define and use specific error types to handle different types of errors.

- Provide meaningful error messages: Include descriptive error messages that provide context about the error and help with debugging.

- Gracefully handle errors: Handle errors in a way that allows the program to continue executing without crashing. Provide fallback mechanisms or alternative paths if possible.

- Log errors: Log errors to the console or a logging service to aid in debugging and monitoring the application's health.

That wraps up Day 23!

Today, we explored error handling and exception handling in JavaScript. We learned about the `try...catch` statement, throwing custom errors, and error handling best practices. Proper error handling is crucial for building robust and reliable applications. Tomorrow, we'll dive into Asynchronous JavaScript and explore concepts like callbacks, promises, and async/await. Keep up the great work, and see you in Day 24.

Day 24: Asynchronous JavaScript

Welcome to Day 24 of "Master JavaScript in 30 Days"!

Today, we'll dive into asynchronous JavaScript. Asynchronous programming is essential for dealing with time-consuming operations like network requests, file I/O, and more. JavaScript provides several techniques to handle asynchronous operations, including callbacks, promises, and async/await.

Topics Covered:

1. Introduction to Asynchronous JavaScript

2. Callbacks

3. Promises

4. Async/Await

5. Error Handling in Asynchronous Code

Introduction to Asynchronous JavaScript:

Asynchronous JavaScript allows us to execute code concurrently, without blocking the main execution thread. This is crucial for handling time-consuming operations and maintaining a smooth user experience. Asynchronous code typically involves callbacks, promises, or async/await syntax.

Callbacks:

Callbacks are a common way to handle asynchronous operations in JavaScript. A callback is a function that is passed as an argument to another function and is executed when a certain event or operation completes. Callbacks can be used to handle the result of an asynchronous operation or to perform additional tasks after the operation completes.

Here's an example of using a callback:

```
function fetchData(callback) {

setTimeout(() => {

const data = "Hello, World!";
```

```
callback(data);

}, 2000);

}
```

```
function handleData(data) {

console.log(data);

}
```

```
fetchData(handleData);
```

In this example, the `fetchData` function simulates an asynchronous operation using `setTimeout`. After the operation completes, it invokes the `callback` function and passes the data. The `handleData` function is the callback function that logs the received data.

Promises:

Promises provide a more structured and powerful way to handle asynchronous operations in JavaScript. A promise represents the eventual completion (or failure) of an asynchronous operation and allows us to attach callbacks to handle the result when it's available. Promises can be chained together and offer better error handling capabilities compared to callbacks.

Here's an example of using a promise:

```
function fetchData() {

return new Promise((resolve, reject) => {

setTimeout(() => {

const data = "Hello, World!";

resolve(data);

}, 2000);

});

}
```

```
fetchData()

.then((data) => {

console.log(data);

})

.catch((error) => {

console.error(error);

});
```

In this example, the `fetchData` function returns a promise that resolves with the data after the asynchronous operation completes. We can use the `then` method to handle the resolved value and the `catch` method to handle any errors that occur.

Async/Await:

Async/await is a modern syntax introduced in ES2017 (ES8) that simplifies asynchronous code even further. It allows us to write asynchronous code that looks and behaves like synchronous code, making it easier to understand and maintain. The `async` keyword is used to define an asynchronous function, and the `await` keyword is used to wait for the resolution of a promise.

Here's an example of using async/await:

```
function fetchData() {

return new Promise((resolve, reject) => {

setTimeout(() => {

const data = "Hello, World!";

resolve(data);

}, 2000);

});

}
```

```javascript
async function getData() {

try {

const data = await fetchData();

console.log(data);

} catch (error) {

console.error(error);

}

}

getData();
```

In this example, the `getData` function is defined as an asynchronous function using the `async` keyword. Inside the function, we use the `await` keyword to wait for the resolution of the `fetchData` promise. The result is stored in the `data` variable, and we can handle it accordingly.

Error Handling in Asynchronous Code:

Error handling in asynchronous JavaScript requires special attention. In promises, you can use the `.catch()` method to handle errors that occur during the asynchronous operation. With async/await, you can use a `try...catch` block to catch and handle errors.

Here's an example of error handling in async/await:

```javascript
function fetchData() {

return new Promise((resolve, reject) => {

setTimeout(() => {

reject(new Error("Error fetching data"));

}, 2000);

});

}
```

```
async function getData() {

try {

const data = await fetchData();

console.log(data);

} catch (error) {

console.error(error);

}

}

getData();
```

In this example, the `fetchData` promise is intentionally rejected with an error. The `try...catch` block in the `getData` function catches the error, and we can handle it in the `catch` block.

That wraps up Day 24!

Today, we explored asynchronous JavaScript and learned about callbacks, promises, and async/await. Asynchronous programming is crucial for handling time-consuming operations effectively. Tomorrow, we'll dive into the Document Object Model (DOM) and learn how to manipulate HTML elements using JavaScript. Keep up the great work, and see you in Day 25.

Day 25: Document Object Model Manipulation

Welcome to Day 25 of "Master JavaScript in 30 Days"!

Today, we'll dive into the Document Object Model (DOM) and learn how to manipulate HTML elements using JavaScript. The DOM represents the structure of an HTML document as a tree-like structure, allowing us to access, modify, and manipulate its elements.

Topics Covered:

1. Introduction to the Document Object Model (DOM)

2. Accessing DOM Elements

3. Modifying DOM Elements

4. Creating and Appending DOM Elements

5. Event Handling

Introduction to the Document Object Model (DOM):

The Document Object Model (DOM) is a programming interface that represents an HTML or XML document as a tree-like structure. It provides a way to access, modify, and manipulate the elements and content of a web page. Each HTML element in the document is represented as a node in the DOM tree.

Accessing DOM Elements:

To access DOM elements in JavaScript, we can use various methods and properties provided by the DOM API. Here are some common methods to access elements:

- `getElementById()`: Retrieves an element using its unique `id` attribute.

- `getElementsByClassName()`: Retrieves elements by their class name.

- `getElementsByTagName()`: Retrieves elements by their tag name.

- `querySelector()`: Retrieves the first element that matches a CSS selector.

- `querySelectorAll()`: Retrieves all elements that match a CSS selector.

Here's an example of accessing DOM elements:

```
// Accessing an element by id

const elementById = document.getElementById("myElementId");

// Accessing elements by class name

const elementsByClass = document.getElementsByClassName("myElementClass");

// Accessing elements by tag name

const elementsByTag = document.getElementsByTagName("div");

// Accessing the first element that matches a selector

const elementBySelector = document.querySelector(".myElementSelector");

// Accessing all elements that match a selector

const elementsBySelectorAll = document.querySelectorAll("p");
```

Modifying DOM Elements:

Once we have accessed a DOM element, we can modify its properties, attributes, and content. Here are some common methods and properties to modify DOM elements:

- `textContent` or `innerText`: Modifies the text content of an element.

- `innerHTML`: Modifies the HTML content of an element.

- `setAttribute()`: Modifies the value of an attribute.

- `style`: Modifies the CSS styles of an element.

Here's an example of modifying DOM elements:

```
// Modifying text content

element.textContent = "New text content";

// Modifying HTML content

element.innerHTML = "<strong>New HTML content</strong>";
```

```
// Modifying an attribute
```

```
element.setAttribute("src", "new-image.jpg");
```

```
// Modifying CSS styles
```

```
element.style.color = "red";
```

Creating and Appending DOM Elements:

We can also dynamically create new DOM elements and append them to the document. Here's an example of creating and appending elements:

```
// Creating a new element
```

```
const newElement = document.createElement("div");
```

```
// Modifying the new element
```

```
newElement.textContent = "Newly created element";
```

```
// Appending the new element to an existing element
```

```
parentElement.appendChild(newElement);
```

In this example, we create a new `div` element using the `createElement()` method. We then modify its content using the `textContent` property. Finally, we append the new element to an existing parent element using the `appendChild()` method.

Event Handling:

JavaScript allows us to handle user interactions and events on web pages. We can attach event listeners to DOM elements to respond to events such as button clicks, mouse movements, and form submissions. Here's an example of event handling:

```
// Attaching an event listener to a button
```

```
buttonElement.addEventListener("click", () => {
```

```
// Code to execute when the button is clicked
```

```
});
```

```
// Attaching an event listener to a form submission

formElement.addEventListener("submit", (event) => {

event.preventDefault();

// Code to execute when the form is submitted

});
```

In this example, we attach an event listener to a button element using the `addEventListener()` method. The listener function is executed when the button is clicked. We can also access the event object and perform additional actions, such as preventing the default form submission behavior.

That wraps up Day 25!

Today, we explored the Document Object Model (DOM) and learned how to manipulate HTML elements using JavaScript. We covered accessing elements, modifying their properties and content, creating new elements, and handling events. The DOM is a powerful tool for building interactive web applications. Tomorrow, we'll dive into JavaScript modules and learn how to organize and modularize our code. Keep up the great work, and see you in Day 26.

Day 26: JavaScript Modules

Welcome to Day 26 of "Master JavaScript in 30 Days"!

Today, we'll dive into JavaScript modules and learn how to organize and modularize our code. Modules allow us to break our code into separate files, making it more maintainable, reusable, and easier to collaborate on.

Topics Covered:

1. Introduction to JavaScript Modules

2. Exporting and Importing Modules

3. Default Exports and Named Exports

4. CommonJS Modules vs. ES Modules

5. Bundlers and Module Loaders

Introduction to JavaScript Modules:

JavaScript modules provide a way to encapsulate and share code between different parts of an application. Modules allow us to break our code into separate files, each with its own scope and dependencies. This modular approach promotes code reusability, maintainability, and separation of concerns.

Exporting and Importing Modules:

To make elements from a module accessible to other parts of our code, we need to export them. JavaScript provides different ways to export elements from a module, such as default exports and named exports. We can then import those exported elements into other modules.

Here's an example of exporting and importing modules:

```
// module.js

export const name = "John Doe";

export function sayHello() {
```

93

```
console.log("Hello, " + name + "!");
}
```

// main.js

```
import { name, sayHello } from "./module.js";

console.log(name); // Outputs: "John Doe"

sayHello(); // Outputs: "Hello, John Doe!"
```

In this example, we have a module file called `module.js` that exports a constant `name` and a function `sayHello`. In the `main.js` file, we import these elements using the `import` statement and use them in our code.

Default Exports and Named Exports:

In addition to named exports, JavaScript modules also support default exports. Default exports allow us to export a single element as the default export from a module. When importing a default export, we can give it any name we want.

Here's an example of default exports:

// module.js

```
const message = "Hello, World!";

export default message;
```

// main.js

```
import myMessage from "./module.js";

console.log(myMessage); // Outputs: "Hello, World!"
```

In this example, the `module.js` file exports the `message` variable as the default export. In the `main.js` file, we import the default export using a different name (`myMessage` in this case).

CommonJS Modules vs. ES Modules:

JavaScript modules come in two flavors: CommonJS and ES modules (ESM). CommonJS modules are the module system used in Node.js, while ES modules are the standard module system introduced in ECMAScript 6 (ES6). ES modules are the recommended approach for modern web development.

CommonJS syntax:

```
// Exporting in CommonJS

module.exports = {

name: "John Doe",

sayHello: function() {

console.log("Hello, " + this.name + "!");

}

};

// Importing in CommonJS

const module = require("./module.js");

console.log(module.name);

module.sayHello();
```

ES module syntax:

```
// Exporting in ES modules

export const name = "John Doe";

export function sayHello() {

console.log("Hello, " + name + "!");

}

// Importing in ES modules

import { name, sayHello } from "./module.js";
```

console.log(name);

sayHello();

While the syntax and behavior of CommonJS and ES modules differ, the concept of modularity remains the same.

Bundlers and Module Loaders:

To use JavaScript modules in web browsers, we often need to rely on bundlers and module loaders. Bundlers, like webpack or Rollup, bundle all our JavaScript modules into a single file that can be loaded by the browser. Module loaders, like SystemJS or RequireJS, provide runtime support for loading modules in the browser.

These tools handle the complexity of resolving dependencies, bundling multiple modules, and loading them in the correct order. They also provide additional features like code minification and optimization.

That wraps up Day 26!

Today, we explored JavaScript modules and learned how to organize and modularize our code. Modules allow us to break our code into separate files, export and import elements, and promote code reusability. Tomorrow, we'll dive into JavaScript frameworks and libraries and learn about some popular options for building web applications. Keep up the great work, and see you in Day 27.

Day 27: JavaScript Frameworks and Libraries

Welcome to Day 27 of "Master JavaScript in 30 Days"!

Today, we'll dive into JavaScript frameworks and libraries. JavaScript frameworks and libraries provide powerful tools and abstractions that simplify the process of building web applications. They offer a structured approach, pre-built components, and additional functionality to enhance productivity and maintainability.

Topics Covered:

1. Introduction to JavaScript Frameworks and Libraries

2. Popular JavaScript Frameworks

3. Popular JavaScript Libraries

4. Choosing the Right Framework or Library

5. Learning Resources

Introduction to JavaScript Frameworks and Libraries:

JavaScript frameworks and libraries are collections of pre-written code that provide a structured approach and reusable components for building web applications. They encapsulate best practices, provide abstractions for common tasks, and offer additional functionality to make development more efficient.

Frameworks typically provide a complete structure for building applications, including routing, state management, and data binding. Libraries, on the other hand, focus on providing specific functionality, such as UI components, data manipulation, or animation.

Popular JavaScript Frameworks:

There are several popular JavaScript frameworks available, each with its own strengths and areas of focus. Some of the most widely used frameworks include:

1. React: A declarative and component-based framework developed by Facebook. React is known for its virtual DOM, efficient rendering, and robust ecosystem.

2. Angular: A full-featured framework developed by Google. Angular provides a complete solution for building large-scale applications, including dependency injection, data binding, and powerful templating.

3. Vue.js: A progressive framework that focuses on simplicity and ease of use. Vue.js offers a gentle learning curve, flexible architecture, and excellent performance.

4. Ember.js: A batteries-included framework that emphasizes convention over configuration. Ember.js provides a strong foundation for building ambitious web applications with a focus on developer productivity.

Popular JavaScript Libraries:

JavaScript libraries offer specific functionality that can be easily integrated into your projects. Some popular JavaScript libraries include:

1. jQuery: A fast, small, and feature-rich library for DOM manipulation and event handling. jQuery simplifies cross-browser compatibility and provides a concise syntax for common tasks.

2. Lodash: A utility library that provides a collection of modular and high-performance functions for working with arrays, objects, and other data types.

3. D3.js: A powerful library for data visualization. D3.js enables the creation of interactive and dynamic charts, graphs, and maps using SVG and HTML.

4. Axios: A lightweight library for making HTTP requests. Axios provides a simple API and supports features like automatic JSON parsing and request cancellation.

Choosing the Right Framework or Library:

When choosing a JavaScript framework or library, consider factors such as project requirements, team expertise, community support, and learning curve. It's essential to evaluate the specific needs of your project and select a framework or library that aligns well with those requirements.

Learning Resources:

To get started with JavaScript frameworks and libraries, explore their official documentation, tutorials, and examples. Additionally, there are numerous online courses, video tutorials, and community forums dedicated to teaching and supporting these technologies.

That wraps up Day 27!

Today, we explored JavaScript frameworks and libraries, which provide powerful tools and abstractions for building web applications. We discussed popular frameworks like React, Angular, Vue.js, and Ember.js, as well as libraries like jQuery, Lodash, D3.js, and Axios. Tomorrow, we'll dive into server-side JavaScript and explore Node.js, a platform that allows us to run JavaScript on the server. Keep up the great work, and see you in Day 28.

Day 28: Server-side JavaScript with Node.js

Welcome to Day 28 of "Master JavaScript in 30 Days"!

Today, we'll dive into server-side JavaScript and explore Node.js. Node.js is a JavaScript runtime built on Chrome's V8 engine that allows us to run JavaScript on the server-side. It provides a robust and scalable platform for building server applications, APIs, and more.

Topics Covered:

1. Introduction to Node.js

2. Setting up Node.js

3. Working with Modules in Node.js

4. Creating a Basic HTTP Server

5. NPM (Node Package Manager)

Introduction to Node.js:

Node.js is a server-side JavaScript runtime that allows us to execute JavaScript code outside of a web browser. It provides an event-driven, non-blocking I/O model, making it highly efficient and scalable. Node.js is well-suited for building server applications, RESTful APIs, real-time applications, and more.

Setting up Node.js:

To get started with Node.js, we need to install it on our machine. Visit the official Node.js website (https://nodejs.org) and download the appropriate installer for your operating system. Once installed, you can verify the installation by running `node -v` in your terminal, which should display the installed Node.js version.

Working with Modules in Node.js:

Node.js uses a module system to organize and encapsulate code. Modules in Node.js are reusable pieces of code that can be imported and used in other files. Node.js supports both built-in modules (such as `http` and `fs`) and external modules that can be installed using NPM (Node Package Manager).

To use a module in Node.js, we use the `require()` function. Here's an example:

```
const http = require('http');
```

This code imports the built-in `http` module in Node.js and assigns it to the `http` variable. We can then use the `http` module to create an HTTP server, make HTTP requests, and more.

Creating a Basic HTTP Server:

Node.js makes it easy to create an HTTP server. Here's an example of creating a basic HTTP server that listens on port 3000 and responds with "Hello, World!" for every request:

```
const http = require('http');

const server = http.createServer((req, res) => {

res.statusCode = 200;

res.setHeader('Content-Type', 'text/plain');

res.end('Hello, World!');

});

server.listen(3000, () => {

console.log('Server is running on port 3000');

});
```

In this example, we import the `http` module and use its `createServer()` method to create an HTTP server. The server listens for incoming requests and responds with a status code of 200, a content type of 'text/plain', and the message 'Hello, World!'. We then start the server and log a message to the console.

NPM (Node Package Manager):

NPM is the default package manager for Node.js and allows us to install, manage, and use external packages and libraries in our Node.js projects. NPM provides a vast ecosystem of open-source packages that can be easily installed and integrated into our applications.

To install a package using NPM, use the following command:

```
npm install package-name
```

This command installs the specified package and its dependencies into your project. The package is then available for use in your code.

That wraps up Day 28!

Today, we explored server-side JavaScript with Node.js. We discussed the basics of Node.js, setting it up on our machine, working with modules, creating a basic HTTP server, and using NPM to manage packages. Node.js opens up a whole new world of possibilities for JavaScript developers, allowing them to build powerful and scalable server applications. Tomorrow, we'll dive into databases and learn about using JavaScript with databases for data storage and retrieval. Keep up the great work, and see you in Day 29.

Day 29: JavaScript and Databases

Welcome to Day 29 of "Master JavaScript in 30 Days"!

Today, we'll explore the world of databases and learn how to use JavaScript for data storage and retrieval. Databases are essential for storing and managing data in web applications, and JavaScript provides various options for interacting with them.

Topics Covered:

1. Introduction to Databases

2. Relational Databases and SQL

3. NoSQL Databases

4. Connecting to Databases with JavaScript

5. Performing CRUD Operations

Introduction to Databases:

Databases are systems for storing, managing, and retrieving data. They provide a structured way to organize and access large amounts of information efficiently. There are different types of databases, including relational databases and NoSQL databases, each with its own strengths and use cases.

Relational Databases and SQL:

Relational databases use tables to store and organize data. They enforce relationships between tables using primary and foreign keys. Structured Query Language (SQL) is a language used to interact with relational databases. SQL allows us to perform operations like querying data, inserting new records, updating existing records, and deleting records.

NoSQL Databases:

NoSQL databases, on the other hand, are non-relational databases that provide a flexible and scalable approach to data storage. They are schema-less, allowing for more dynamic and unstructured data. NoSQL databases come in various types, such as document databases, key-value stores, columnar databases, and graph databases. Examples of popular NoSQL databases include MongoDB, Redis, Cassandra, and Neo4j.

Connecting to Databases with JavaScript:

JavaScript can interact with databases using database-specific drivers or libraries. These drivers provide APIs and methods for establishing connections, executing queries, and handling the results. Some popular JavaScript libraries for working with databases include:

- **For Relational Databases (SQL):**

- Sequelize: A promise-based ORM (Object-Relational Mapping) for Node.js that supports various SQL databases such as MySQL, PostgreSQL, SQLite, and MSSQL.

- Knex.js: A query builder for Node.js that supports multiple SQL databases and allows you to write SQL queries in a JavaScript-friendly syntax.

- **For NoSQL Databases:**

- MongoDB: A popular NoSQL database with a native Node.js driver that provides a straightforward API for interacting with MongoDB databases.

- Redis: An in-memory data structure store that can be used as a NoSQL database or a caching system. Redis has a Node.js client library for easy integration.

Performing CRUD Operations:

CRUD (Create, Read, Update, Delete) operations are the fundamental operations performed on databases. Here's a brief overview of how these operations are typically performed using JavaScript:

- **Create:** Insert new data into the database using an INSERT statement or a database-specific method provided by the driver or library.

- **Read:** Retrieve data from the database using SELECT statements or methods provided by the driver or library. You can specify filtering conditions, sorting, and other criteria to retrieve specific data.

- **Update:** Modify existing data in the database using UPDATE statements or methods provided by the driver or library. You can specify the columns to update and the conditions for selecting the records to update.

- **Delete:** Remove data from the database using DELETE statements or methods provided by the driver or library. You can specify the conditions for selecting the records to delete.

It's important to refer to the documentation of the specific database and JavaScript library you are using for detailed information on performing CRUD operations.

That wraps up Day 29!

Today, we explored using JavaScript with databases. We learned about relational databases and SQL, NoSQL databases, connecting to databases with JavaScript, and performing CRUD operations. Databases are a crucial part of web applications, and JavaScript provides powerful tools for interacting with them. Tomorrow, we'll dive into asynchronous programming in JavaScript and learn about callbacks, promises, and async/await. Keep up the great work, and see you in Day 30, our final day.

Day 30: Asynchronous Programming

Welcome to Day 30, the final day of "Master JavaScript in 30 Days"!

Today, we'll explore asynchronous programming in JavaScript. Asynchronous programming allows us to execute tasks concurrently, improving performance and responsiveness in web applications. We'll cover various techniques, including callbacks, promises, and async/await.

Topics Covered:

1. Introduction to Asynchronous Programming

2. Callbacks

3. Promises

4. Async/Await

5. Handling Errors in Asynchronous Code

Introduction to Asynchronous Programming:

Asynchronous programming is a programming paradigm that enables non-blocking execution of tasks. It allows tasks to run concurrently, making efficient use of system resources and improving the responsiveness of applications. JavaScript, being a single-threaded language, heavily relies on asynchronous programming to handle time-consuming operations such as network requests or file I/O.

Callbacks:

Callbacks are a traditional approach to handle asynchronous operations in JavaScript. A callback is a function that is passed as an argument to another function and is invoked once the asynchronous operation completes. It allows us to specify what action should be taken after the operation finishes.

Here's an example of using a callback to handle an asynchronous operation:

```
function fetchData(callback) {

// Simulating an asynchronous operation

setTimeout(() => {
```

```javascript
    const data = 'Some data';

    callback(data);

  }, 2000);

}

fetchData((result) => {

  console.log(result);

});
```

Promises:

Promises provide a more structured and intuitive way to handle asynchronous operations in JavaScript. A promise is an object that represents the eventual completion or failure of an asynchronous operation. It allows us to chain operations and handle success or error conditions easily.

Here's an example of using promises to handle an asynchronous operation:

```javascript
function fetchData() {

  return new Promise((resolve, reject) => {

    // Simulating an asynchronous operation

    setTimeout(() => {

      const data = 'Some data';

      resolve(data);

      // Or reject(new Error('Some error'));

    }, 2000);

  });

}

fetchData()
```

```
.then((result) => {

console.log(result);

})

.catch((error) => {

console.error(error);

});
```

Async/Await:

Async/await is a modern approach to handle asynchronous programming in JavaScript. It provides a more synchronous-like syntax and simplifies the code structure. The `async` keyword is used to define an asynchronous function, and the `await` keyword is used to pause the execution until a promise is resolved or rejected.

Here's an example of using async/await to handle an asynchronous operation:

```
async function fetchData() {

return new Promise((resolve, reject) => {

// Simulating an asynchronous operation

setTimeout(() => {

const data = 'Some data';

resolve(data);

// Or reject(new Error('Some error'));

}, 2000);

});

}

async function fetchDataWrapper() {
```

```
try {

const result = await fetchData();

console.log(result);

} catch (error) {

console.error(error);

}

}

fetchDataWrapper();
```

Handling Errors in Asynchronous Code:

Error handling is an important aspect of asynchronous programming. It's crucial to handle both synchronous and asynchronous errors properly. In promises and async/await, you can use the `catch` method or `try/catch` blocks to handle errors gracefully.

Additionally, many asynchronous functions and libraries provide error callbacks or reject promises with specific error objects to provide meaningful error information. Always refer to the documentation of the specific library or function you're using for error handling details.

Congratulations!

You've completed the "Master JavaScript in 30 Days" challenge. You've learned essential JavaScript concepts, explored various topics, and built a strong foundation in JavaScript programming. Keep practicing, building projects, and exploring new technologies to further enhance your skills.

Thank you for joining this journey, and I wish you continued success in your JavaScript endeavors.